What Would YOU Do?

Discovering a New World

Would You Sail with Columbus?

Elaine Landau

Enslow Elementary
an imprint of

 Enslow Publishers, Inc.
40 Industrial Road
Box 398
Berkeley Heights, NJ 07922
USA

http://www.enslow.com

Enslow Elementary, an imprint of Enslow Publishers, Inc.
Enslow Elementary® is a registered trademark of Enslow Publishers, Inc.

Library of Congress Cataloging-in-Publication Data

Landau, Elaine.
  Discovering a new world : would you sail with Columbus? / by Elaine Landau.
    pages cm. — (What would you do?)
  Includes index.
  Summary: "Readers decide if they would sail with Christopher Columbus, and then find out what really happened"—Provided by publisher.
    ISBN 978-0-7660-4222-3
  1. Columbus, Christopher—Travel—America—Juvenile literature. 2. America—Discovery and exploration—Spanish—Juvenile literature. I. Title.
    E118.L35 2014
    970.01'5092—dc23
                    2013008786

Future editions:
Paperback ISBN: 978-1-4644-0387-3
EPUB ISBN: 978-1-4645-1213-1
Single-User PDF ISBN: 978-1-4646-1213-8
Multi-User PDF ISBN: 978-0-7660-5845-3

Printed in the United States of America

052014 Lake Book Manufacturing, Inc., Melrose Park, IL

10 9 8 7 6 5 4 3 2 1

To Our Readers: We have done our best to make sure all Internet Addresses in this book were active and appropriate when we went to press. However, the author and the publisher have no control over and assume no liability for the material available on those Internet sites or on other Web sites they may link to. Any comments or suggestions can be sent by e-mail to comments@enslow.com or to the address on the back cover.

♻ Enslow Publishers, Inc., is committed to printing our books on recycled paper. The paper in every book contains 10% to 30% post-consumer waste (PCW). The cover board on the outside of each book contains 100% PCW. Our goal is to do our part to help young people and the environment too!

Photo Credits: ©Clipart.com: pp. 20, 28 Enslow Publishers, Inc. using ©Artville, LLC. Images, pp. 15, 42; iStockphoto.com/©mesaphoto, p. 4 Library of Congress, pp. 1, 8, 38, 41, 43; National Oceanic and Atmospheric Administration (NOAA)/Photo: FGBNMS/Eckert, p. 19; Shutterstock.com/©Ashiga, p. 16; ©Thinkstock: (Dorling Kindersley RF, pp. 10(cross-section), 30, 36; Peter Bull, p.10(top); Jupiter Images/Photos.com, p. 12; Peter Dennis, pp. 23, 24; David Schrader/iStock, p. 33; Photos.com, p. 34).

Cover Illustration: ©Thinkstock: Dynamic Graphics/liquidlibrary

Contents

Statues of the great explorer Christopher Columbus stand in many places around the world.

A New Idea

The Time: 15th Century
The Place: Europe

What an exciting time! Explorers and seafarers in Europe longed to travel to new lands. They wanted to see new sights. They dreamed of returning with gold, jewels, and other riches.

The East Indies was on everyone's mind. There were many wonderful things to find there. Tea, rare spices, and pepper were just a few. There were also silk, gold, silver, and jewels.

Going to the East Indies by land was difficult and dangerous. It took months. The trip traveled through long stretches of desert. Bandits robbed travelers along the way as well.

A speedy sea route to the East Indies was needed. And an Italian sea captain named Christopher Columbus had one in mind. He hoped to reach the East Indies by traveling west. He and his crew would go across the Atlantic Ocean.

But there was one problem. Two large land masses blocked the way. These were North and South America. But Europeans, including Columbus, didn't know about these lands yet.

The trip Columbus planned would cost a lot of money. He would need the help of a royal to do it. First he asked King John of Portugal for help. But King John turned him down.

Next he went to Spain. But things didn't go well there either. They were at war against the Moors in the southern tip of Spain. They needed money to build up their Navy. There would be little left for exploration. It took a year before the king and queen even agreed to see Columbus.

What Would YOU Do?

What would you do if you were Columbus?

※ Would you give up and go home? Time has passed. You still have nothing to show for your idea.

※ Would you come up with a new dream to go after? It's the 1400s. There are still plenty of places to explore.

※ Would you go to France? You might have better luck there. Maybe the King of France will back your plan.

Columbus meets with the King and Queen of Spain to ask for money for his trip.

Columbus Refuses to Give Up

Columbus clung to his dream. He did not leave Spain. After six years, Queen Isabella finally gave him the money he needed. She was not alone in her choice. Some Spanish nobles also believed in Columbus.

Columbus was now the admiral of a fleet of three ships. Columbus planned to sail on the *Santa Maria*. That was the largest and most sturdy vessel. The other two ships were the *Niña* and the *Pinta*. Both were smaller and lighter ships. The crew on these

This cross section of the *Santa Maria* shows how crowded the ship was.

boats would be especially cramped. Most of the men would have to sleep on straw mattresses on deck. The men would even have to sleep in shifts.

The captains on the *Niña* and *Pinta* were brothers. Vicente Yanez Pinzón would be in charge of the *Niña*. Martín Alonso Pinzón would be captain of the *Pinta*. Columbus had met with both men ahead of time. But after spending some time with Martín, Columbus knew that he didn't like him.

Martín was hungry for glory. This worried Columbus. He feared that Martín might try to take credit for the mission.

Yet Columbus needed Martín Alonso Pinzón. Martín was a more experienced and better known seaman than Columbus. He was respected and even had some ships of his own. Martín would be useful in getting crew members to sign up.

Did the *Niña, Pinta,* and *Santa Maria* ever set sail?

What Would YOU Do?

What would you do if you were Columbus?

- Would you ship out with such small, overcrowded ships? Would you feel okay about leaving with a captain you didn't fully trust?
- Would you insist on finding another captain to replace Pinzón? This might delay the trip. Pinzón was also very well liked by sailors. It might be harder to put together a crew without him.

The Trip Begins

Columbus decided to set sail. Things were not perfect. But on August 3, 1492, his small fleet left from the Spanish seaport of Palos. Their first stop was the Canary Islands. They'd restock their supplies there. The 89-man crew would need more meat, cheese, fruit, and water.

But that wasn't all they needed. Soon there was a new problem. On August 6, the *Pinta* sent a message to the *Santa Maria*. The smaller ship's rudder had loosened from its mounting. On August 9, the *Pinta* arrived at one of the Canary Islands. By then the ship was disabled and badly leaking.

Wind shifts stopped Columbus's other two ships from reaching that island. A few days later, they arrived at another one of the Canary Islands. Meanwhile the *Pinta* crew had tried to repair it but failed. The ship needed a new rudder. It couldn't sail on without one.

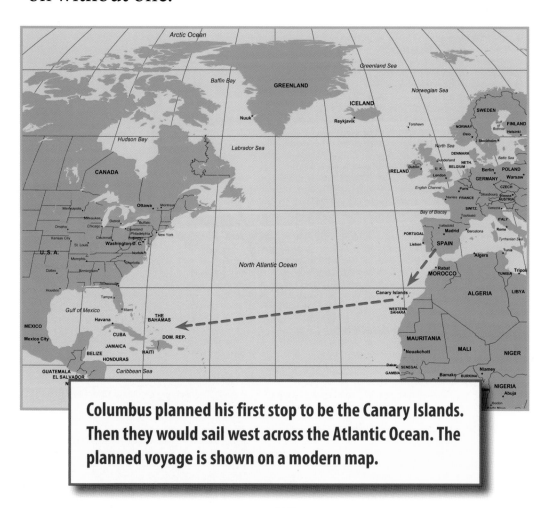

Columbus planned his first stop to be the Canary Islands. Then they would sail west across the Atlantic Ocean. The planned voyage is shown on a modern map.

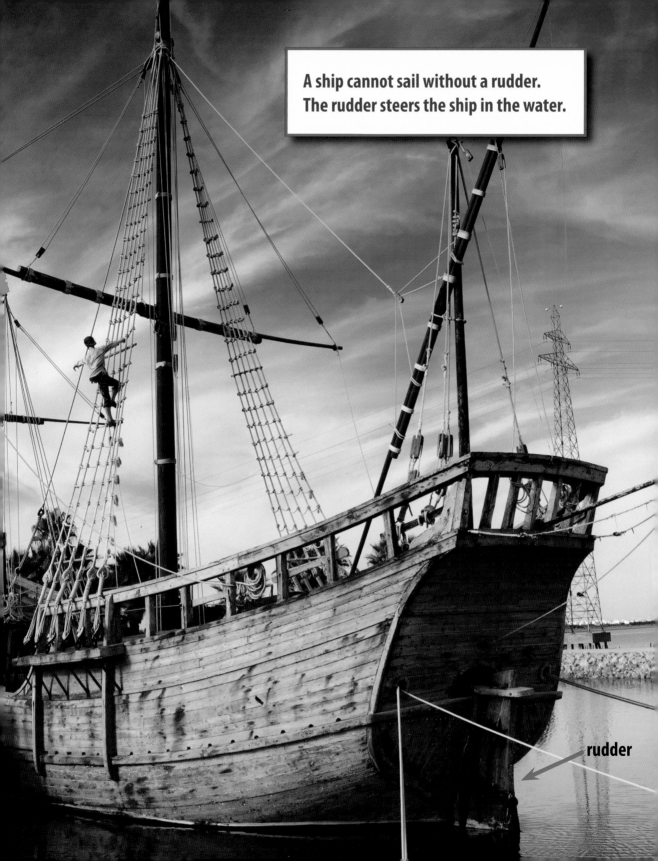

A ship cannot sail without a rudder.
The rudder steers the ship in the water.

rudder

What Would YOU Do?

What would you do if you were Columbus?

✳ Would you leave the *Pinta* in the Canary Islands and sail on without it? Then you'd have fewer ships and men for the trip.

✳ Would you visit a few nearby islands? You could look for a ship to replace the *Pinta*.

✳ Would you wait where you were until a new rudder could be built for the *Pinta*?

Columbus Finds a Way

Columbus knew he needed the *Pinta*. He could not make the trip with just two ships and fewer men. So he had the men build a new rudder for the *Pinta*. But this delayed the trip for three weeks. They did not leave the Canary Islands until September 9.

Columbus didn't count on further problems. But there was trouble ahead. After leaving the Canary Islands, the crew became lonely and scared. They were sailing a course they had never been on before. They hadn't seen land in a long time. They wondered if they'd ever see Spain again.

Then before long the men grew really frightened. The water around them was suddenly filled with thick floating grass. They thought they might get trapped in the vast seaweeds.

Today we know the men were not really at risk. The ships had merely reached the Sargasso Sea. That's an area in the North Atlantic Ocean. The green weeds are from the algae plants there. But Columbus and his crew couldn't have known this.

Columbus's ships entered the Sargasso Sea, which was full of thick seaweed.

Columbus was a determined admiral of his fleet.

Many of the men wondered why they had ever set out with Columbus. They asked him to change course and head home. But Columbus refused.

That is when the whispers started. Some men began to plot against Columbus. They thought about throwing him over-board. They'd make up a story to cover up the murder. Some wanted to say that he fell from the ship while checking their course by the stars. Then the men would try to get home without him.

Columbus got wind of the plan. He was worried but determined. He was still admiral of the small fleet. He would not turn back even though his life was now in danger.

What Would YOU Do?

What would you do if you were Columbus?

※ Would you have the troublemakers whipped and kept in chains?

※ Would you come up with a story to calm the men —even if the story wasn't completely true?

※ Would you not allow the men to talk together in groups after work? That might make it harder for them to plot against you.

A Clever Trick

Columbus had to calm the crew. If the men felt safe, Columbus knew he was safe. Then the voyage could go on.

So Columbus wrote up a false daily log book. He put down a smaller number of miles in it than were really traveled each day. This was the only log book he showed the men. It made them think they were still fairly close to home. This stopped their grumbling for now.

Yet the trip didn't go smoothly for long. The *Niña* and the *Pinta* were lighter, quicker ships than the *Santa Maria*. That meant they were often ahead of Columbus's boat. At times, it was hard to keep the

Every day, Columbus wrote a false log book entry.

fleet together. Columbus told the Pinzón brothers to slow down their ships. He did not want the vessels too far from one another.

The *Pinta*

But Martín Alonso Pinzón had other ideas. On September 17, he sped ahead on the *Pinta*. Columbus didn't like this. He still didn't trust Martín. There was good cause for this. Martín wanted to be the first to spot land. The Spanish King and Queen had offered a large reward to whoever spied land first. Martín Alonso Pinzón wanted both the money and fame.

Columbus caught up to the *Pinta* at about sundown. Martín Alfonso Pinzón was waiting for him. He told Columbus that he had spotted land about 45 miles to the north.

What Would YOU Do?

What would you do if you were Columbus?

❁ Would you listen to Martín Alonso Pinzón? Would you change course and head north on his advice?

❁ Would you stick to the course you're on? Martín Alonso Pinzón had sailed the seas many times. But you've done some sailing too. You don't think there's land in that direction. Should you just sail on as planned?

Where's the Wind?

Columbus did not listen to Martín Alonso Pizon. He felt sure of the direction he was headed in. He would stick to the course until there was a good reason to change.

Yet Columbus still had to deal with the crew. Most of the men were upset again. Now they were unhappy about the wind. Suddenly the sea had become very calm. It looked like a sheet of glass. The men were unsettled. Many complained night and day. Without the wind, the men thought they'd surely be stranded at sea. They feared being left out on the ocean with no way to ever get home. It wasn't what they'd dreamed of or expected.

What Would YOU Do?

What would you do if you were Columbus?

- Would you try to reason with the crew? Maybe you could explain how wind and water currents work. You could also say that they were probably getting closer to land. Water tends to be smoother near land.

- Would you try a different approach? You might think that a scientific answer would not work for the crew. You could simply tell them that the still water was an act of God. You could say that prayer is the answer and ask the men to pray.

Columbus told the men not to worry.

Moving Once Again

Columbus told the men not to worry. He said that God was not punishing them. He also asked the men to pray for wind. Columbus promised that everything would be fine before long.

This seemed to work. Luckily, the wind soon began to blow. The sea picked up and the crew felt the boats move. Now they were as calm as the sea had been before. And when they felt calm, Columbus was safe from harm.

Other good things began to happen as well. Some small birds were spotted. This is a sign that land is near. Several whales were seen as well. The men knew that whales usually swim near a coastline.

Did Pinzón really see land this time?

Then on September 25 something really exciting happened. Just before dusk, Martín Alonso Pinzón called out to Columbus. He claimed that he had seen land. He also claimed the reward that the King and Queen of Spain had offered to the first man who spotted land.

Had Pinzón really seen land this time? Did it mean that they had finally reached the East Indies? Columbus hoped so. He dropped to his knees on the deck and thanked God.

What Would YOU Do?

What would you do if you were Columbus?

❁ You didn't see the land yourself. Should you trust Pinzón and change course to reach the land he said he saw? You think this area may be about 75 miles southwest. But you're not sure. Would it be wise to change course now or should you keep heading west? You were right not to change direction before.

❁ Should you stay on course until you see proof of land yourself?

A Few False Starts

Columbus decided to take a chance. He changed his course. By September 26, he was heading southwest and hoping to find land. It was a mistake. What Pinzón saw was not land after all. He had only spied some squall clouds. These can look like land at times.

Columbus righted his course. By that afternoon, he was again headed west. Yet the crew was still quite upset. The men had really hoped that land was nearby. Now they weren't sure anymore.

Then on the morning of October 7, some men thought they saw land to the west. So the *Niña* was sent speedily ahead to see. But their hopes were soon dashed. Once again, the sighting turned out not to be real. By now the men were more upset than ever. They were determined to turn around and go home. They didn't care if Columbus was in charge. They were about ready to rebel and take over.

Was that land in the distance or just some clouds?

Would Columbus avoid a mutiny with his crew?

What Would YOU Do?

What would you do if you were Columbus? At this point Columbus was not in a good place. He knew that land was near. Yet he knew he'd never see it if there was a mutiny.

✳ Would you be firm with the men? Maybe you could stress all the signs of land you'd seen. You could remind them that you are still the admiral of this small fleet. The men are duty bound to follow you.

✳ Would you just lie to the crew? You could tell the men that if you didn't reach land in a few days, you'd turn the fleet around. Then all of you would head home together. Though you would never really do this, it could buy you some time.

A sailor spies land.

Safe!

Columbus played it safe. He told the crew he would turn the fleet around if they didn't reach land in a few days. Things calmed down for a bit.

Meanwhile, there were some other good signs. Branches with flowers were seen in the water. One even looked like a carved cane.

On October 10 at about 10:00 P.M., Columbus thought he saw a light. Could it be a fisherman's torch? Columbus was not sure of what he saw. He asked others to watch for the light.

About four hours later, a sailor named Rodrigo de Triana really spotted land. He shouted out the good news. He also fired off a signal to let everyone know.

Land! The crew sees the New World for the first time.

What Would YOU Do?

What would you do if you were Columbus?

❋ Would you be happy for Rodrigo de Triana? As the first to spy real land, he would get the reward promised by the King and Queen of Spain.

❋ Being Columbus, would you feel that only you should get the reward? After all, the voyage was your idea from the start. You could say that the light you saw earlier was the first real land sighting. Then you could keep the reward for yourself.

Success!

Columbus claimed the reward for himself. But what really excited him was finally reaching land. After setting foot on dry earth, Columbus dropped to his knees. He kissed the ground and thanked God.

Columbus thought he'd landed on an island off the East Indies. But he was wrong. He was really in what is known today as the West Indies. The natives there had never seen a white person before. They thought Columbus and his men might be gods.

For the most part, the natives were peaceful people. They lived in huts and grew their own food. Sadly, Columbus did not respect the natives. He forced them to work for him for free. He also made them become Christians. That was not a proud time in history for Columbus.

When Columbus landed, he claimed the land in the name of Spain. He kneeled on the ground and was thankful.

Columbus did not stay where they had landed for long. He was an explorer and was always on the move. Columbus still thought that he was near the Asian mainland. So he explored quite a few nearby islands.

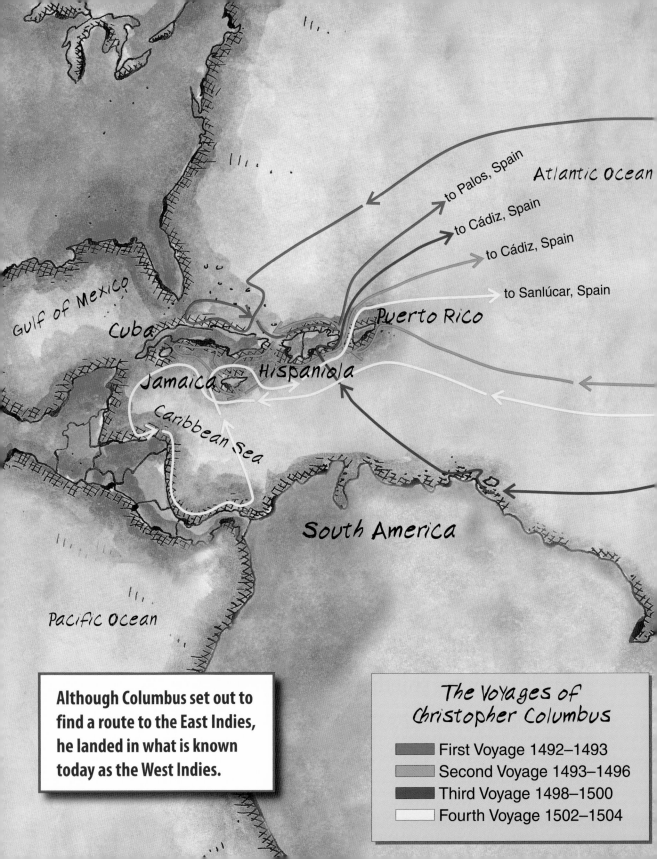

to Palos, Spain Atlantic Ocean

to Cádiz, Spain

to Cádiz, Spain

to Sanlúcar, Spain

Gulf of Mexico

Cuba

Puerto Rico

Hispaniola

Jamaica

Caribbean Sea

South America

Pacific Ocean

Although Columbus set out to find a route to the East Indies, he landed in what is known today as the West Indies.

The Voyages of Christopher Columbus

First Voyage 1492–1493
Second Voyage 1493–1496
Third Voyage 1498–1500
Fourth Voyage 1502–1504

Christopher Columbus returned to Spain and visited with the royals.

But on Christmas Eve 1492, the worst happened. The *Santa Maria* crashed on a reef near Haiti. The ship split apart. Columbus could not use the vessel in that condition. So he left about 40 men with the ship to try to repair it. They were also told to search for gold in the area.

Then on January 16, 1493, Columbus began the trip back to Spain with the rest of his crew. Now

Columbus captained the *Niña*. His rival, Martín Pinzón, was on the *Pinta*. Pinzón reached Spain before Columbus. But the royals refused to see him. They were waiting for Columbus. They did not have to wait long. Columbus reached Spain on March 15, 1493. The royals were very proud that day.

Columbus was not ready to stop exploring. Between 1492 and 1504 Columbus made four voyages westward. He explored parts of Cuba, Jamaica, Puerto Rico, South America, and other places. He always hoped to find a westward route to the East Indies but he never did. Finally, he gave up on the idea and returned to Spain. Columbus died on May 20, 1506 in his home there.

After Columbus's first voyage, people looked at the earth differently. They saw that the world was much bigger than they thought. It also had a lot more water. This not only changed mapmaking. It further opened the world for explorers.

Timeline

1492

August 3: Columbus's three ships set sail from the Spanish seaport of Palos.

August 9: The Pinta arrives in the Canary Islands. At that point the ship is badly disabled.

September 9: After a three-week delay, Columbus leaves the Canary Islands. A new rudder has been built for the Pinta. Now the ship is in good shape again.

September 26: Columbus changes course and heads southwest. Martín Alonso Pinzón thought he saw land in that direction. Columbus hopes to find it, but there's no land there. Columbus adjusts his course back.

October 10: At about 10:00 P.M., Columbus spots a light. He thinks it might be the torch of a fisherman in the water but he isn't sure.

October 11: At about 2:00 A.M., sailor Rodrigo de Triana spots real land. He fires off a signal to let everyone know.

October 12: Columbus goes ashore after finally reaching land.

Words to Know

admiral—A naval officer of high rank.

bandit—A robber or outlaw.

continent—Any of the world's large land masses, such as Europe or South America.

course—The route or direction taken by a ship.

crew—A group of people who run a boat.

current—A body of water moving in a definite direction.

fleet—A group of ships.

land mass—A large area of land.

log book—The official record book of a ship.

Moors—A group of Muslim people who invaded Spain in the eighth century.

mutiny—An open rebellion by sailors at sea.

rudder—A flat piece used to help steer a boat.

seaweed—A type of plant growing in the ocean.

squall cloud—A light gray rolling cloud that's usually beneath a dark cloud mass.

vessel—A craft for traveling on the water.

Learn More

Books

Aloian, Molly. *Columbus Day.* New York: Crabtree, 2010.

Bodden, Valerie. *Columbus Reaches the New World.* Mankato, Minn.: Creative Education, 2010.

Freedman, Russell. *Who Was First: Discovering the Americas.* New York: Clarion Books, 2007.

Gifford, Clive. *10 Explorers Who Changed the World.* New York: Kingfisher, 2008.

Mann, Charles C. *Before Columbus: The Americas of 1491.* New York: Atheneum Books for Young Readers, 2009.

Markle, Sandra. *Animals Christopher Columbus Saw.* San Francisco: Chronicle Books, 2008.

Nelson, Robin. *Columbus Day.* Minneapolis, Minn.: Lerner Books, 2010.

Web Sites

Explorers for Kids. Christopher Columbus.
<http://www.ducksters.com/biography/explorers/christopher_columbus.php>

National Geographic Kids. History: Christopher Columbus.
<http://video.nationalgeographic.com/video/kids/history-kids/christopher-columbus-kids/>

Index